Circular Breathing

For Maggie,
Richard, Donald and Gerald

Circular Breathing

Poems by Graham Mort

DANGAROO PRESS

Acknowledgements

Kunapipi, Poetry & Audience, Poetry Review, Nimrod (USA), Stand, Iron, Poetry Wales, Outposts, An Idea Of Bosnia (Feed The Children anthology), Sunk Island Review, Tees Valley Writer, Scratch, Acumen, 'Marigolds Grow Wild On Platforms' (Cassell anthology), 'Century' (Orbis anthology), 'Pennine Tracks' (Pennine Poets anthology), BBC Radio 3 'Between The Ears', Poetry Society Web Site.

'Black Market' won a Duncan Lawrie prize in the 1994 Arvon Foundation International Poetry Competition.

'A Quiet Bloke' was a prizewinner in the 'Highly Commended' category in the 1996 National Poetry Competition.

Many thanks to the Society of Authors for the Authors' Foundation Award which helped me to work on this collection.

Thanks to Anne Collett for her careful reading of the manuscript

Cover painting 'Carp' 1997, by Jan Coventry

Author photograph © K. Jelley

Dangaroo Press gratefully acknowledges the financial assistance of Yorkshire and Humberside Arts Board

© Graham Mort 1997

This book is copyright. Apart from any fair dealing for the purpose of private study, research, criticism or review, as permitted under the Copyright Act, no part may be reproduced by any method without written permission. Enquiries should be made to the publisher.

First published in 1997 by Dangaroo Press
PO Box 20, Hebden Bridge, West Yorkshire HX7 5UZ, UK

ISBN 1-871049-43-1

Printed in Great Britain by Villiers Publications, London N3

Contents

Imagining The Woods At Katyn	1
Today	2
Runaway	4
A Quiet Bloke	6
Spiders	8
Imperatives	10
Flymowing	12
Quarryman	14
Black Market	16
Samurai	18
Girl At Long Lane	19
Waiting For O'Malley	20
First Born	21
Earlsferry	22
A Riddle For The Serbian Wars	24
Duet	25
Southbound	26
Bees	28
Dandelions	30
Wall Riders	32
The Ice Cream Man	36
Storm Larks	38
The Guest	39
Time, Love & Tenderness	40
Inheritance	42
Laxton's Superb	44
Blackout	46
Neighbour	48
Travelogue In Circular Breathing	50
The Gig	52

Bidean Nam Biam	54
Fox	57
The Dream Of The Circus Dwarf	58
A House Of Glass	61
Moonwalking	70
Machair	72
Remembering Dunblane's Children	74
Valentine	76
Wardlock	78
Mannequins	80
Hysterectomy	82
The Hurts	85

Imagining the Woods at Katyn

Rain is in my hair, it is bending
back leaves where the pale mouths
of convolvulus implore a silence.

A finger-bone lies at my feet,
its fine nib glistening in the rain,
writing and re-writing the same story.

I've brought a white handkerchief,
empty pockets, the clay of another
country smothering my boots to

this place where God forgot himself
again, closing his eyes so that
the rain would not fill them.

The woods tease my ears with brotherly
whispers of comfort; there is a stink
of leaf-mould and sour uniforms.

A collared dove follows her cry into
this silence, pecking at young
mushrooms which glow like skin in

the clearing where they knelt,
hands snared in prayer,
the pistol barking at their necks.

Spiders tie their gauzes everywhere:
over the iridescence of tyre-ruts.
onto leaves that shiver still.

Rain is in my hair and I am tangled
in its blue veils, stumbling across
the forest's unmerciful frontiers of light.

Today

Today the fields steam-up a bleating sunrise;
lambs are picky-toed on their heat.

A ginger cat strolls over rooftops
filching nestlings from the chimney pots;
her tail stiffens to an electric rod
of fur at the jackdaws' hiss.

The first swallows perch shoulder to shoulder,
divining insects that swarm below the wire;
their throats swell in lipstick kisses.
A man free-wheels home his brother's bike,

his widow watching from the lattice
where clematis trails; spokes mill the light
into cruelties of remembrance, spanners jostle
in the saddle bag and the chain is hoarse.

A car starts first time, coughing politely,
smug in its blessed miracle of parts –
one virtuous life in a sinful congregation
of blown head-gaskets and exhausts.

The newscaster's voice updates us:
the situation in Ecuador, then Janáček;
his violins are urgent as sparrows
soaring in a giddy flock of notes.

That vapour trail scribes its curve
from a silver compass-point;
it wavers, gives up measuring,
then skids into ski-tracks of smoke.

There's the cat again, licking its paws,
shivering from the bloody taste of soot,
there's the glint of coffee in these cups,
sanpaku, that sudden mooning of an eye.

There's a blue vein crossing your hand,
the pulse of moment passing into moment,
there's Ecuador, Janáček, that sunburst
gasping across a wall as the clouds spill.

Runaway

Back at base we put the record straight,
scald our throats with sweet tea,
sweat out the relief of finding nothing
and tell it how it was.

How ice broke under us as we tiptoed
the path's brink of frozen mud, our torchlight
hewing that hut from the dark, our
breath dulling its padlock's frost.

How little there was inside:
a hemp rope, an oil can, the reek
of tar and diesel, spent cartridges,
newspapers, white rigging repairing
windows with its trembling yarn.

How cattle bellowed behind us, then
a fox yelped, how the farm's stub glowed
as wind sucked it and how we heard the echo
of that name they kept throwing at the dark.

We say how we stood listening
and how the stream would not hush
itself across the earth's curve;
how a pheasant crackled from the woods
and the sky cleared as we squinted
for satellites, bringing the Pleiades
from their fading-trick of light.

In the morning they'll let dogs sniff
at her clothes then track her.

They'll find her huddled in that nook
of larches, still breathing, dribbling
a miracle of ice from the thumb in her mouth,
only an hour from the big sleep.

Or she'll be covered with a sheet
where the flashlight sprawled her,
the forensic squad on their hands and knees
prising clues from leaf-mould and fingernails.

Right now we're in the pick-up driving home,
empty-handed, sleepless, thinking of bleak
headlines and black waters, of a figure
who might still drag herself from the trees
towards her father's litany of all
she had to stay for.

Needles jab and flicker on the dials,
measuring each stammer of wheels on a track
where headlights stun the sheep, bounce
from night's meniscus of sky, then
find the road and sweep it clean.

A Quiet Bloke

He was a quiet bloke, retired groundsman
at the county pitch, unmarried, childless –
the way these things are measured –
but troubled by something enough one day
to take the spade from a neighbour edging
geranium beds, down him in one, then slice
off his head, methodical as digging turves.

He went home, changed his spattered shoes
then gave himself up like a crossword clue,
muttering how he'd suffered leylandii long
enough, how bowlers followed through straight
down the track, which wasn't on, how things
build up, get worse, go unremarked –
how twenty-two yards make a chain.

Detectives checking the neighbour's trees saw
how they'd stolen away the church clock;
and sure enough, they didn't find a timepiece
in the house, even checked the quiet bloke's
wrist for the white band a wristwatch leaves, found
nothing except the sinew that years of grass mowing,
seed sowing and marking out with lime had knotted.

A reporter swore the quiet bloke smiled when
the pathologist ascribed to him some knowledge
of anatomy – he meant the way the bloke had
slipped that spade between vertebrae and turkeyed
the neighbour's head – even so, it was a gory mess
that left the jury faint, one police photographer
checking out his pension dates, the press swabbing
copy from that overgrown suburban lawn.

At the trial the quiet bloke showed no remorse,
offered no defence; he waved on sight screens
when sun dazzled the courtroom, asked for a brushing
and heavy roller at recess and, when weather broke,
greeted the usher by counting overs lost through rain;
but mainly he was the quiet bloke he'd always seemed.

As he said himself that time, chilling the duty officer
with calm reserve, things build up, go unremarked;
but on receiving sentence we noticed how he seemed
to glance down at his wrist, to bite his lip, then cast
his hand in a slow circle from the dock as if remembering
something he'd practised or always meant to do.

Spiders

The spiders stayed awake again.

I call you and you leave the bed
to see: at work all night
wiring up the apple trees,
the windows, the angles
of the broad bean canes,
all aerialised for some broadcast
far beyond our frequencies.

Their threads gleam like fishing line
disappearing into the air's depth,
melting in the sun which has risen
again to burn off the dew, dust shadows
from under roofs, shape-shift hills
that smoulder in heaps of cooling slag.

Spiders' reproaches are everywhere:
Work! Work! Work!
each one a steeplejack welding
his steel filaments to a frame,
a tight-rope star burnishing her own
glittering steps above the night.

They know how to wait
and how to betray,
how to say nothing and lie still,
how to seem a shadow of shadows
a silence of the silence,
how to look away whilst looking on;
their eyes multiply the frail-winged
prizes of the day.

They are hidden and waiting –
everywhere –
for that first faint touch
to bring them unblinking to the light.

It comes: expected, surprising
as my mouth reaching to kiss
pale hair on your neck's curve,
sudden as your tears, stopped
on my unbuttoned sleeve.

Imperatives

Rise to one whiskey glass growing
stale, the bottle horizontal
as if you'd spun it for luck,
true north or nakedness.

Discover one letter on the mat,
morning light sprawled across
its postmark, the front gate clacking
behind the postman's step.

Shave now, wince at that splinter
in your hand which only hurts
when you remember it and probe
its sliver of steel or thorn.

Gulp coffee, go to work leaving
the bed unmade, the window open,
tapping gently like Blind Pew's stick
or a stylus clocking a forgotten groove.

Now think of coming back tonight –
of breathable emptiness – then remember
how you first arrived, hoisting
her across the threshold as a joke.

Consider the irony of things
half-built – unopened tile grout,
the shower kit from B & Q, the wall
lights' bouquets of lethal wire.

Work because work numbs your mouth
like novocaine, like sleep numbs an arm
or the fuse-box numbed your hands
that time the lights went down.

Wake again tonight, hearing cats howl
at the multiple sins of sex, imagine
how chestnut trees hissing on the hill
could be tropical surf or snakes.

At breakfast find the same letter,
unopened, propped against the salt,
its invoice of hurt outstanding
and indelibly specified.

Let sunlight on the wallpaper remind
you of pageboy hair, its gloss
when she opened the fridge, humming
a tune's unfinished bridge to things.

Watch the toaster lob flaming slices
onto melamine and through the smoke observe
a bluetit hover at the window, momentarily
exotic, a suburban hummingbird.

Stare where its wings and your eyes blur,
to where the days lie down in rows
and only the joker is set aside
in their unfinished game of solitaire.

Now junk the deck and swear
you never lied.

Flymowing

Flymowing the lawn all summer
was hell.

I had to keep on at it
while the grass grew like fire
and she lay upstairs
with whatever it was
coming inside her; so long
since I'd touched her, I'd
forgotten how.

No matter how much you keep it
down it grows after the least
bit of rain – that June
we had a drenching and then
the sun driving it on.

It was madness – like bloody
Vietnam – and the cats wild
for the young birds all summer.

At night I dreamed of it – eternal,
slopes of green and me alone
hacking at it with just the edges
of my hands;
she'd be asleep or lying
listening to what I muttered
about grass, about two-stroke,
the pull-start stalling.

Sometimes I thought of it
inside her, hollowing her eyes,
but that shadow was the shadow
of something growing;
one night I found myself on the lawn,

groping without a moon to see by
and weeping for something lost,
there in the grass, lost.

After thirty years you don't
talk much or can't.

Each time I'd check for stones
on the newly laid bits she'd
wanted: easy to bend a blade
or jam up on a piece of stick –
everything stops then.

Flymos?

Flymos are a bastard to start.

Quarryman

On Friday nights they'd jive to Palais bands:
red Epiphones, a tenor sax, the bass guitar
booming through black speaker cloth,
a drum-kit spangled by the drummer's hands.

Egged on by mates who'd watch, half-pissed,
he'd climb the stage to sing for her,
the band in waltz-time but rock and roll
already nudging their slow rhythms with its fist.

Now each Friday, in a fried stink of chips,
he slams the kitchen table, shouts, insists
he'll be the master in this house of whores,
his spittle flecking bloodless lips.

When his song of anger hits full pitch
the kids cower at the tv, pretend it loud
enough to staunch the sour ejaculate of words
that sates him as she never could, *the bitch.*

But this time she hurls back her voice's hate
to see him flinch at wormwood he's distilled,
until she's running from the house into the dusk,
through their rank garden to the kissing-gate.

She flees the path, pants into trees, afraid
to meet lovers or the lonely men with dogs;
the quarry-face is pink with sunset's haze,
the town below a hive of dozing bees.

She turns from hurt as she would turn a page
well-thumbed from over use, knowing by heart
how her cheek will turn from red to blue,
her skin the litmus of his rage.

Her breath grows shallow, she's dipped in light –
the last gold that the day will see. Glossed
in song she hears a warbler liquefy the sun,
these notes their way of counting in the night.

On the path the young slugs glide in pairs –
black, purposeful, they hunt their kin
and somehow orchestrate their lust to kill –
a rabbit screams out from the keeper's snare.

The iron gate creaks open, red with rust,
white moths haunt woodsmoke, flicker at her knees
as she goes home to find him weeping in a chair,
the voice that wooed her choked with dust.

Black Market

It's dawn and the river steams.
He waits for you by the bridge – as they
said he would – his feet gently stamping
on the snow's crust, next to the chestnut
seller, that newsvender breathing smoke.

You sidle up to him, this zek-head
in the long coat: no salute,
you greet him with one word and hear
your own language harsh in his mouth.
No names, no pack-drill.

His eyes water in their red slits,
his lashes blinking at the cold or
at poverty. He licks a stained moustache,
his tongue furtive behind the cigarette;
already his inattention cheats you.

You are wearing your good shoes, your
warm jacket quilted against the cold
as your head is quilted against the hour
by last night's drinks. At the bar you boasted
of leaving, the whole city turning under your heel.

He thumbs the white crescents of his eyes,
a rat slicks across dead nasturtiums, sleek
as the river where it goes under the parapet.
The man gestures *follow*, his hand an exclamation,
his nails filthy with secret work.

He smells of wet wool, stale books, of dead
philosophy, of something you want or meant
to get round to in the end but never did:
he squats in your head and his name
cannot be written down or evicted, ever.

He is your blind date, waiting as you are.
You'll follow him into the city, into
basement cafes where the soup is thin and sour,
into tanyards and shop fronts where the deals
are struck – each one, someone's bad bargain.

Nothing goes as planned. One job you said,
wanting to be on a flight, counting dollars,
seeing a softly torn sea below, curving palms,
a catamaran far out and a beach-house where
cool women are sipping rum spilled over ice.

Now you've got packets hidden in the floor,
daren't answer the phone, or that late-night knock.
The landlady's eyes are black with sudden hate
and her face shows you what you are. Today
you rang a friend and the line died.

Tonight they'll hand you an address, a bridegroom's
photograph – enough to know him at close range –
something wrapped in oiled cloth, its chambers
clicking in your hand. Then used notes, half now and
half later. Then moments ticking themselves empty.

Samurai

Your blouse left out
to dry across the grass
is pale blue – enough to stitch
a sailor's pocket –
but grey clouds are curling
in to spoil the sun.

A horsefly stings my arm
and pulses there
armoured in silk and plate,
a bronze samurai
hunching, lazy
in the drowse of blood.

Now you're there, stepping
from the lilac's shadow
to ask me something,
your toes pressing the grass,
asking with urgent words as
a red nipple blotches my wrist.

The horsefly's wings blur
where it stumbles
dazed on its burnished
scaffold of legs.
Your hand is on my arm,
your question singing in my ears.

Last night I dreamed
our son had died,
but look, he's there now
in the doorway, unsteady,
scolding the grass and scowling
like a stone.

Girl at Long Lane

The track slots into the hills' vee,
white with dust and the white hope
of leaving.

Grass tears under the teeth of sheep;
her shoes click on the path, polishing
its flat stones.

A cuckoo suckles the wood's
green air; she counts each quaver,
steps into the day's light.

Thistles spike the garden;
at dusk they bloom with moths,
with pale wing-beats.

Last night the wine of her dream
was apple-scented, its slush of ice
trickling on her tongue.

Today the farmhouse sweats steam
and woodsmoke; dance-hits billow
from the radio.

She steps over hens where they cluck
in the dirt, laughs at bees drunk
again in the foxgloves.

She drops the basket from her hip,
lifts her father's shirts into the sun
and sings.

Waiting for O'Malley

My orders are to wait for O'Malley
then stiff him in any corner of this field
that's cold as a promise never kept,
foreign and windswept as a Belfast alley.

Furrows are unfreezing from the night,
curving into a dawn raw as the eyes
of sleepless squaddies, glazed with frost
and thaw and gusts of icy light.

A flock of goldfinches feeds on thistle heads,
their down glossy as a brochure of somewhere
far away. We watch the track where he will come,
imagine the path he treads.

The goldfinches stare and peck
and peck and stare like blind prophetic
birds of stone; they glean harsh oracles
of peat-water that gurgle faintly from the beck.

These co-ordinates are mapped in O'Malley's
head; he knows where the cache is, which target,
when. The sun is bitter as cordite, bright
as the copper that jackets lead.

A kestrel hovers: wing-tips blur
to hold it still as it interrogates
the land for movement, searching
for indiscretions that give its retinas a kill.

Each moment of the waking day
we think of him and without hate, knowing
that he'll come stepping soon into our sights
we're anxious, as if a loved one was late.

Our fingers are stiff and frozen to the bone,
our breath is white as fusillades of river mist.
This is the kind of duty no one likes –
the kind of duty that must be done.

First Born

First, a song I'd never heard,
tolling through green light,
now this shell in my back's hollow
rocking me to the edge of space.

I tread moss, wool, nest-shit;
the egg draws me up then dimples
off into air's clamour of cold –
one less, one less, one less.

My little mother comes again,
squirts grub-fat under my tongue;
she gives warmth stupidly, broods
me all night, her own chick,

the quick black ball of her eye
too worry-blind to question.
That scream in the air is mine
it goes out from my skinny chest

and will not stop. But she's
too small too soon, crooning
the wrong song at my back
to stuff me full of fury.

Who can know their own nature?
Hunger is what I am and thirst,
needy for lodging and heat under
a foreigner's stinking wing.

Today something changed, that voice
at the edge of things beating up
pure bubbles of blood in my throat.
This territory is ours for the taking –

I shiver where a quiver of new
feathers pricks at my skin;
soon I'll know who and why
I am. Soon we will begin.

Earlsferry

'Hard to find unless you know
what you're looking for...'
No irony here, just wind and water-light:
you might have spent years on a beach
like this, stooped under the breeze,
shadowed by a white sun, your eye
deciphering salt-glazed fragments of shell,
your brown feet slipping on belts of weed.

There's a jellyfish dying on the sand,
purple with venom, clear as an eye's lens,
stinging nothing but the passing heat
and this passing crabmeat stink.
Your hand scatters armoured claws
across sand, nudges water-ridges,
seizes what is here by some momentous
chance or diligence of the sea.

They're miniature slugs – slimeless,
calcified – grooved as gramophone records,
storing the North Sea's analogue of tides
for playback to the future's hearing.
They're pursed mouths, half smiling,
half in pain; flushed pink, dainty as new
shoots or tender cunts: my fingers would
bruise them or thwart their budding.

Behind us, our footprints ooze
toe-shaped mirrors of cloud;
four oil-rigs moored on the firth,
driftwood bleached at the tideline,
herring gulls loitering, terns
slanting down-wind then slashing
the sea, a judiciary of cormorants
on that black promontory of rock.

Hard to find, this currency of the undertow:
perhaps a dozen on any beach, and we
have eight, bleeding water into your hand.
We count them again, standing above
rock pools which flicker to stillness,
each one fermenting a new version
of tomorrow for a coastline which butts
the sky in dwarf-hunched hills.

We hold our hands under water, let
them touch like drifting fish bones;
the sun falls and its flattened light
catches your eyes for a moment, blue as dusk.
We turn to go and a seal appears, far out,
slick as basalt, nosing from the sea's sheen
of lost whale cries and fished-out shoals,
fluxing the silvers of a breaking tide.

A Riddle for the Serbian Wars

I am smoke curling from the cannon's mouth
a cockerel's white feather

I am the cry of women, the keening
shell that falls into a town's sleep

I am the roof beams burning
and the cellar's huddled dark

I am the poem in a rapist's mouth
the rictus of hanged men

I am this hushed breathing
this shrinking prayer this litany of lies

I am the speck in a neighbour's eye
that covets your thistled acre

I am a white eagle, a white dove
a white face pressed to the wire

I am the knock at your door
the torchlight checking your face

I am the soldier's unsheathed pride
the slurred song of a nation

I am the cartographer drunk on ink
my hand on the pen the trigger the pulse

I am the question glinting at the border
the black stamp across your name

I am a dumb witness a twisted tongue
a language pecked out and sung by crows

Who am I?

Duet

Today the wind is in the piano, zithering
until bichords and trichords almost hum –
the way I almost whisper you my dream,
its diminuendo of passing years.

One day the wind will sing like this
and leaves will fall into your violin
the way autumn fell on your hair
and silvered it, the way it breathed
onto your manuscripts and scrolled
them into yellow curls.

You lie under the days' mysterious light
understanding only the air, its gavotte
in the piano's polished case, its easy
ebb and flow as your wrist bows slow
notes towards life, future, or something
like it that my fingers search for.

The wind quavers in our dream of days,
this illusion of anticipation and accord
still in our heads where violin and piano
tread fine legato footsteps; downstage
we see to things beyond brocade curtains
and intent faces, things which soon we only
hear and then a tune we half remember,
fumbling for notation, key and tempo.

Even now we hardly hear it.
No applause, but my hands at your temple,
soothing it without haste or words because
the wind has dried our mouths, surprising
us with things still left to say, because
your eyelids lifting leave me reading clear
grey grace-notes where I know I'll never
stop looking or hearing us begin.

Southbound

Last night we went missing from
the world, had to drag sleep's
drowning to surface for this train,
southbound, late and slow as a cortège.

Pigeons flocked into apricot clouds
from the station's roof of glass;
we walked the platform, rolled newspapers
into wads and thumped our legs.

Now there's rain, the train swishing
over sleepers, the conductor reciting
his poem of destinations, warming each
town's cold consonants Jamaican-style.

At Warrington chimneys spindle
the mist, spinning hanks of smoke;
the track's drawn threads gleam under
a gnawed moon's waning into day.

Those travellers watch us and wait,
their breath white, their faces
vague as ingots cooling in a tank.
We judder on the squeal of brakes,

slip into the suction of gathering light.
A woman eats her yoghurt with a silver key,
a man spins a yellow pear,
that girl sleeps with folded hands

and will wake soon to make her face.
Rain flecks the windows, slakes
dried sorrel in fields below where
a white mare runs by the fence

flicking back her head
from the brink of our din.
A signalman stares from his lit box,
hands parting the track, neat

as sugar tongs to send us south.
The conductor's voice comes again, its hymn
sing-song and sorrowful, pronouncing each
place's name until we're almost sure it's there.

Bees

It was the year when bees dropped
everywhere, stalling on the air
to lie like felled half-backs,
their wings faintly groaning,
their striped shirts brassy
with lost speed.

Why that year of all years
was hard to say and saying
it printed headlines in the papers,
got neighbours talking on doorsteps,
kids filling jam-jars with
those clots of bumbling wings.

We saw them falling too, drawing
their front legs overhead, cleaning
away something we couldn't see, mired
in honey or nectar or sheer remorse –
typical of me, you said, to make a bee
feel guilt.

Somehow we failed to draw
the right parallels: their
spinning from the clover heads
and our inability to stop anything
happening anywhere –
especially here, where a quarrel
could waste mealtimes like a wind
of flames in eucalyptus.

We drew a blank on the fall
of the bees, but fielding
at cover-point I'd see one
there at the popping crease,
inches from the batsman's boots,

risking each stroke to wallow
in pleasure or in pain.

It was hard to tell ecstasy
from agony or ritual;
taking the piss, you said,
watching one rise and fly away
into a full-stop.

But it went on: peg out a line of shirts
and a bee would be there in the yard,
knackered from overtime on the
gorse blossom shift, semaphoring
mad narratives of nectar
in its dance, trying to rise
from stones the sun had parched.

Or you'd be ducking a low-flying jet,
swallowing its dry roar,
and notice that you'd trodden one
onto the road, its purpose spilled
and sticky, the seconds it occupied
flowing away, its flight-paths
lost as forgotten place-names.

There was a glut of foxgloves,
that year, the shadows of bees
in purple bells; we imagined pupae
swarming, a fat queen smug in royal
jelly, workers falling from the air
that you were pumping into a bicycle
tyre when one stung you on the wrist.

For no reason, you said,
turning, biting out the poison
sac, telling me to leave,
or that you would.

Dandelions

They'll grow anywhere, dandelions,
their seeds flocking to a mist,
swarming in faint dreams of light
from a far dimension of Space,
weaving the sheer silk of air
and staining it to watered milk.

They settle on our shoulders,
on the roofs of cars or houses,
on gravel paths or by the roadside;
you wouldn't rate their chances higher
than icicles in hell.

But in spring they come through:
obvious things forgotten, which suddenly
are remembering themselves everywhere,
rising through damp soil and cold and rain,
through fretted autumn leaves,
the lengthening days' light.

They take over garden paths,
flower beds, verges, window boxes;
they punch through tarmac in the street,
their tap roots spiking into graveyards
to rock the headstones, their faces
brightening the names of the dead.

The first flowers I took my mother
were dandelions,
snapping a fistful of stems,
their sap trickling down my wrist,
sticky as sperm,
their yellow heads oozing a faint
scent of piss and bitterness.

I smelled the space between their lives
and mine.

This one clings to the outhouse roof,
gulping in heat from the May sun
with grateful little nods,
downy as a new duckling,
its baby head lolling
in a faint breeze
that teases it to fall.

Tomorrow's wind will strip you,
tear out that gloss of fibres,
your bald pod drying to a husk,
your root slumbering between slates,
under winter stars – their suddenly
blooming flowers of frost.

In spring you'll pull the house down,
or try to.

If I'm here and you make it,
I'll come down one day, woken by
the hunger of starlings, taking in
today's milk from the doorstep,
yesterday's news from the paper,
to find you, suddenly overripe.

Wall Riders

The pavement opens up to take us down,
spilling its scree of steps to a kiosk
where that silent woman palms our coins
and the turnstile clicks, licking
the tickets from our hands;
down there a red light guards us,
its ruby glistening in the tunnel's mouth.

We're swallowed in this underworld
of trains, their chrome and steel gleam,
their hiss of rubber silencing the line:
the Paris Metro's squealing tonnage
and sudden doors, its voltage numbing
the rail to blackness, near enough
to reach and put an end to touch.

The train leaves as we arrive,
a fairground ride that vanishes
our shadows with its temporary light;
they press back from darkness as the night sky
would behind a comet's tail of fire and ice.

But this is Paris by night, its curve
of track and sleeper, its stations' names
plotting a city's prodigal wakefulness.
Its cafes scatter neon across the river's
water-foils, its citizens' faces
are miniatured in each raised glass.

A train shudders-in, doors thudding
as we board to ride the line into the north.
Your hand collides with mine, wheels spider
the current, smoothing out brief turbulence
and whining over shoals of sparks.
Our knuckles burn, white
as children's faces at a window.

Suddenly, beyond everything that's near –
tangible and permanent – she's at our lips
and we are speaking her into this air.
There in the cancer ward back home,
sleepless in a metal bed, under white sheets
and an English sky of rain clouds. Beyond
chalk cliffs, the Channel, that ketch
we saw ploughing with its kite-tail of gulls.

We are between stations in the dark,
our faces fuzzy in the window glass,
thinking of her and of her father,
booted and leather-zipped on his Tiger Cub,
laughing at gravity's poor propositions,
riding that typhoon of planks each night
and strobing striped canvas to a blur.

She told us how she watched the crowd
hail the living myth of him –
his face Christ-pale and saintly –
suspending him in their held breath
as we balance her now in ours, ready
for applause to break into the hush.

At Pigalle night air is hot as sweat;
it stinks of piss and Galleoises.
A beggar turns in rags and papers
on that bench; her friend the busker sings,
one tooth needling the treble of lost love.

The Sacre Coeur is white as lime,
its crowds swarm and murmur, their
babble of tongues curious and profane.
They turn their faces to the basilica
or to the sun where it falls, fusing
the lit switchboard of the city.

Inside, points of flame scent
and scorch a dimly rising space,
its vaulted lung coughs echoes
into shadows restless with prayer.
The faithful kneel before the host
in its tabernacle,
its bread made flesh,
its miracle of wine unbled.
The candle we light for her melts
into a mask of wax, not quite faithless
nor quite hopeless, but guttering
and flaring still.

The city's domes are leafed golden
by the lights, moored boats nudge
the Seine, their hulls whispering
under the bridge where that man's
wine-glass orchestra might be playing still,
Bach's cantata coaxed from moist rims,
his fingers christening their humming crystal.

At Notre Dame each leaping beast launches
a stony anguish at the night and cannot
be soothed by God's nearness, nor by
the moon rising, steady as an anchor-fluke:
it calls into her window, white as
morphine that soothes each day
with space enough for pain to drift
towards our voices at the outer edge.

We've walked for miles and can't go on:
streets rise up to the hill of martyrs
or fall to the river, taking us towards
tomorrow when traffic will wake the boulevard
and revellers curse homewards, still drunk
enough to blame their spellbound feet.

We slide into the underground again,
its sigh of compressed air inhaling us
as easily as dust; we wait, then take
the train, bracing as it bucks the current,
longing for sleep, not looking back, but
hollow-eyed as shades in all its trembling glass.

Your fingernails are polished
by the steel they curl around,
your face, already only half-awake,
sways as we slow down, shipped
under the river homewards, or to
somewhere we'll call home tonight.
The train rocks then quickens:
Trinité, St. Lazare, Madeleine,
each station measuring the dark with light.

The Ice Cream Man

Here comes the evening ice-cream man,
turning the hurdy-gurdy higher,
nudging the kerb with the ice-cream van:
we hear the squeal of its fat black tyre.

Is it that his eyes are too yellow,
the hair on his arms too coarse and rough
to play the part of the ice-cream seller?
When he speaks his voice is low and gruff.

But he greets the children with a kind *hello*,
scooping their wishes from the frozen tub;
he warns them of traffic and watches them go,
his lips sucking smoke from a cigarette stub.

The children who queue there do not know
that his mind is a darkened cinema
where old Pathé newsreels flicker and glow:
the salute, the eagle, the swastika.

He has a whole shelf of books on the Reich,
a patent black leather belt and boots,
a model machine-gun, a motor-bike,
and a wife whose hair is blonde to the roots.

He watches the Führer speak each night,
the uniforms massed in the heaving stands;
when applause explodes the pigeons to flight
they wheel like a flock of clapping hands.

And he's even clapped his own hands numb
at meetings held in those secret places
where real-life fascists from Germany come
to help cleanse the country of non-white faces.

Under the counter where he puts the coins
are photographs taken through Belsen's wire:
the skeletal ribs, the wasted loins
excite him with itchy sweats of desire

that make his shaking hands clench tight.
The needle of hate is climbing the dial
and we see, as the dusk turns into night,
what he means by that feral ghost of a smile.

The street is empty, the blinds are rolled,
but he plays the music for one more taker,
his fingers are bruised purple with cold –
like the butcher, the baker, the candle-stick maker.

Storm Larks

Sky is black as a ciné film spooling its last
reel; imageless, burned by the light, its
white-gashed celluloid flickers overhead.

The horizons tremble, then stand still,
accepting the warm rain; our breathing falters,
uncertain as purple in the sun's fading bruise.

This frequency is all wow and flutter and rumble
on the earth's slow platter, its grindstone
flinting out split-second streaks of light.

The gleam across your face fixes it here:
white, ecstatic with shushed exclamations –
then bass notes beginning below hearing's octaves.

It's ironic we don't think of God now, only
of the ions colliding, those fronts of heated air
and copper dousing-rods drinking an electric blue.

But it's death-sky music, you said so,
your hand on mine glimpsed as a claw of bones,
so old it could be winged or scaled, half-human.

Lightning fuses air's nitrogen, cattle stumble
awash in curdled milk; ponies' eyes panic,
their mouths foaming at rain's polished bit.

The voltage goes to ground, missing the uncoiled helix
of acids that wash away, futile for a billion years
until the chance of it lights like a struck match.

We're sheltering by this gable-end, watching
the town blitzed to monochrome, seeing skylarks stall
then fly on singing into the air's stunned height.

The Guest

You're waiting for something here
and know what but dare not say,
saying instead how beautiful the light
through the last beech leaves,
how good to be here again
in her town garden
with the exiled fig tree,
the laburnums and all
the windows of the house
switched on by an October sun;
you're waiting for something
and the hostess takes
your hand and you grip hers
just long enough to feel
her fine bones, to hear
the tinkle of her laughter
falling unbreakably;
you're waiting as the sun
tilts on the wine in your glass,
imagining his mouth on her bare
shoulders, then on yours,
knowing that his tread on the lawn
will come at any moment, trembling
and scattering opal seeds of dew.

Time, Love and Tenderness

In this suburb of the city we stop
at the Wheatsheaf for a drink,
just where the B-road drops us
after the motorway and poppy fields
where lapwings skim the cars' hot roofs.

Cooler in here and dim at first:
we order cold beers, lean on bar towels,
hear pool balls click in their triangle
of noon's lubricious light.

The jukebox is hushed, repeating
the same song like a wish:
Time, love and tenderness
over and over in this tap-room
tiled like a piss-house and kippered
with last night's smoke.

We're not complaining: it's the right
place to be right now, right here where
there's nowhere else. The optics wink,
brimful of whiskey and gin, of vodka
and five-star forgetfulness.

Dust sequins the air. A rod of light
comes in like something you could touch.
A girl in stacked heels coils a snake-
bite into her belly, shoots pool with that
hobbling man, laughing, tilting her cue
into the table's alluvial green.

Her child bawls from its pushchair,
arms waving to some comfort beyond reach,
her tongue searching for speech until
silenced with a crisp.

From a side-table a youth looks on,
conjuring the future from one slow beer.
Cyclists pass the open door, wind
hustles litter on the street, blowing
the day away into the sun's high curve.

The song whispers, wistful, conniving
as they range the balls onto the felt;
she picks the child's milk from the floor
like a bottled cloud, or bottled love
or time or tenderness, wiping its teat
on her red dress.

The limping man cues the phalanx.
It slicks wide open and he grins as balls
fall from cushions into pockets – like money
or virtue or luck never did into his.

The landlord takes our glasses, leans
into another haze of lunchtime drinking,
hearing the jukebox's psalm anoint us,
seeing the angles of light fall more narrow,
the hot road glitter as we turn to leave.

Inheritance

He watched the first snowflakes abseil
into the yard's stink, melting on dung
he'd forked there, making the farm dogs
whimper, yelp, snatch at their chains.

That morning lapwings had dropped into the fields,
surprising him with their jester's flight:
too early for spring, the wind was in the north
and each bud a blackened tip of steel.

The week before he'd watched cherry blossom
in the graveyard. Now this wind would strip each
branch to its filament, its wake of frost
clamp shut the throats of crocuses.

Last night the sun had fallen slobbering
at the red lips of clouds, pleading
to be out into the bloody world;
it sank unheeded and with it sank the light.

Then the wind had moved a compass point,
its anticyclone whorling over the North Sea,
bringing its inheritance of cold to dull him –
like uncashable war-bonds, the Fordson, the land.

It frayed his knuckles where he worked the fields'
need of him, walling up gaps where frost
and thaw had shunted stone downhill
to let his pregnant ewes stumble through.

It froze the promise in his mouth, stung
him with hailstones' unrelenting kisses.
She was in the valley, bellyful of his child,
a thin acre of this farm already sown in her.

That night, alone, he cradled his head
at the fire, smelling sweet muck dry in its heat;
alone, letting the wind go over the fell,
the river glitter towards imagined cities.

He went outside to lean against a solid wall
of cold, blinking the Plough's stars from his eyes,
letting the door creak on its hinge of light,
his breath drift, white as a moth's flight.

Laxton's Superb

Back home we are younger than we should be:
our faces years less cynical and open with hope,
these photos fading in the hallway light where
rosaries hang handy for the Sunday dash to mass.

We wake in separate beds, under the abundant
quilt of their forgiveness and today the sun is early,
rising as your father used to for his shift,
the shunting yards gonged by steel slammed

into steel, the men downing tools, banning
overtime at grudged pay or fairness, cooking
bacon on a shovel in the loco's furnace-heat
like Lucifer pictured in a book.

The bypass beats bird-song to the day, its tape-
loop hissing in the idle focus of our hearing,
tea-cups chink downstairs, the sky's bell-jar
numbs the suburbs in a carbon daze.

Your father fills the kettle, spoons tea from
the coronation caddy and whistles-in the day;
we hear the water rise and fall, soft as Irish tides
he dreams each night will wash him home.

Sun is already burnishing traffic, the multiple eye
of the greenhouse, the empty washing line,
someone flushes the plumbing and it fills the tank
with whispers that peter out in small amens.

Over your bed the saints send their eyes to heaven,
there's a palm-leaf cross, your mother's harsh
catechism of breath extolling sleep's virtue
from the next room, and we dare not touch.

In the garden potato leaves are yellow;
the drills crumble, rhubarb is dusty
with drought, toads shrink from the heat,
their living blisters hidden under stones.

The apple trees planted for each child are bright
as candelabra in the sun, each sprig of leaf curled by lack
of rain, each circling wasp drunk on sugar and the sticky
hum of wings, each fruit hanging ripe and bitten.

Blackout

Imagine how I felt after all we'd seen.
He'd count the years of life he'd missed,
settle on that night in '40, heading north
with a trainfull of airmen, mainly pissed.

They loved their uniforms, the fucking war.
After fifty years, conviction he was right;
each station dim as a closed chapel,
each town moving blindly towards night.

At Wigan a squad of MP's walked the train,
their boots clobbering the corridor,
they took a stammering sailor-boy who wept
and couldn't answer questions any more.

The squaddies jeered as at a mis-kicked goal,
the KO punch that robs a loser of his legs;
he saw searchlights stab the dark, the pass
sweated in the pocket of his battle-dress.

Then the sky began to glow, reddening
like a million sucked-on NAAFI cigs,
dusk still dropped incendiaries of dark,
the East End burned around his digs.

A mine had razed the house next door,
an off-duty nurse recovered, dead;
invisible coils of smoke unfurled
their acrid sermon in his head.

The carriage filled with little gasps,
then voices muttering, slurred, half tight,
the train shuddered in to Manchester
which blazed in a yellow rage of light.

It hollowed out the night sky's pith,
the glass from windows cracked and fell,
hoses were varicose, the gutters streamed,
baptised each back-lit gate of hell.

Heat itched the khaki on his neck,
a police sentry waved him on; he spat
smoke's emetic from his mouth,
the city crackled-up like bacon fat.

He turned his back upon the fires,
his kit-bag slung to leg it home
towards a house that might be blitzed
by some Heinkel's ironic surplus bomb.

He followed the tramlines' polished steel –
seven miles of marching quite alone,
towards a future he could not guess
but ached for like a fever in the bone,

towards stars he'd never seen before
and could not name, above the town.

Neighbour

Today a man comes knocking at your door,
his laughing face is hidden in his hand,
his pale eyes shift like eyes of sand.

Birds snatch winter berries from the wind,
wires sing, their slow hymns drifting
over blown-flat fields of snow.

The man brings nothing except a face
stripped bare, hands empty
of everything but laughter's snare.

Trees shake off the yellow brevities
of spring, tremble in the first dearth
of winter's siege and suck at the earth.

The man welcomes you to your own home,
to this country you thought was yours;
you note his soft, familiar way with words.

Sky blanches to a precipice your blood
can't climb or pass; snow lies against
window-ledges, whispers on glass.

The man cancels refusals from your face;
he conjures papers and conceals a gun, he
offers you terms on this house you own.

At once you see a dream of this:
lines of pilgrims in trudging streams,
lice following a warm shirt's seams.

The man switches all the house lights on,
he sighs into a fireside chair, he draws
you close and strokes your hair.

Outside a wren jerks its agate eyes,
jabbing at the rowan fruit's red rind
where washing stiffens in the wind.

Soon you'll walk from the house and turn
from the land, you'll run from every stick
and stone and every neighbour's hand.

The man shakes his head, regretting
the trust he placed in you, not laughing now
but needling a number on your arm in faintest blue.

Travelogue in Circular Breathing

Dolan driving to another job balances the map
on the steering wheel, changes down for the ring-road,
for another sales-pitch steepening with every year of soft-
soaping a living from discount stores, bars and corner shops.

He parks on the gravel forecourt: another hotel with
oil-sump breakfasts and plastic en-suite bathroom doors,
no vacancies, but tv's left on all night by legless
middle-managers asleep in crumpled suits as snow
falls on the town and the river blackens the weir.

Dolan drops his bag, pisses, yawns into the mirror, stares
through curtains to check his watch against the only local
legend here: four church clocks keeping four wrong times.

Dolan brews up an instant tea, adds whitener, thinks
of cows drooling to milking parlours through the frost
of churned fields, their burning breath figuring a woman
in jodhpurs he used to fuck on a farm when he was younger
in a bigger car, her old man harvesting peas as they sweated
in bed, working at a climax like he'd work at sales figures
or persuasive charm.

That last time she'd slammed the door, white-faced,
whispering *go away*, away because her life had crashed
back into place where it belonged under the neighbours'
gossip and glaucous, potato-picking eyes; he knew why
that came but never how.

Dolan lies down, relishing breast-weight and buttock-
curve, her neck and perfume, her wet mouth on his
and cries for more in summer heat that sent them crazy,
upturning furniture and bedroom rugs. Dolan trying to
remember hugs the pillow where the smell of someone
else's cigarettes not quite laundered from the sheets
tugs him to the present moment on its leash.

He needs a drink. No problem – anything he wants here
where he's known by name, another balding rep in striped
shirts and cheap shoes, his car lined up outside with the others
like wives over-dressed for functions where the men are given
golf-clubs, gold watches or holidays in Spain for simply being
where they had to be and doing what was done.

Dolan in the bar feeling smaller and older than he should
is secretly twice the man these younger bastards ever were,
boasting of iron-pumping, blowjobs and fuel injection in
voices sadder than that fifty year-old child's in the hostel across
the street, yodelling at the night like a dingo or didgeridoo –
on and on, Jesus, on and on – which reminds Dolan
of circular breathing, that someone once told him the way
the trick was done; exactly how he's forgotten now, but
still feels pride in something once known.

Traffic goes past in the rain, the sound of someone sweeping
a floor or sanding a box; headlights slide across the ceiling
of room seven, searching for something or someone lost.
Dolan shifting to switch on the news spills tea down his shirt,
dabs it with the bedspread that smells of smoke, hearing
the man-child's broken voice howl down a fat moon from
cloud-gaps over the hostel garden.

Later, in the Chinese takeaway Dolan watches goldfish
circling in a tank, wondering if the woman he saw yesterday
shaking rain from her hair at a bus-stop is still there some-
where, as the fish spiral, finning the glass and sucking up
the gravel with oriental calm, until he's tired of their slow,
exotic ease, of hearing the girl with black hair and eyes, no
older than his own daughter and too polite to shout, asking
him over and over, round and round, what he wants, please.

The Gig

The band vamp menace, strut their stuff,
count triplets to the closing chords,
stage-lights flicker to a shagged-out blues,
the singer's lips ooze scarlet words.

The lights are blindly vague, smoked
air translucent as the singer's shirt,
cymbals gong the Les Paul's skidding
halt in valve-hot, over-driven dirt.

Their toiling drummer towels sweat;
the bass-player kills the PA's hiss,
the singer whispers faint *fuck yous*
at punters rising for a final piss.

They slash on dog-ends, pools coupons,
on useless fucking teams who never won –
whiskey chasers and the silent howl
of failure make them dumb.

The sax player flicks spittle from his reed,
the drummer shakes his head and farts,
their set-list drifts from unsold tapes
towards that final, losing round of darts.

The barmaids' eyes are ringed with black,
the barman fires down one last short;
each beer pump is shrouded now, like
murder suspects bundled into court.

Taxis pant into the streetlamps' glare,
a cat's-eye moon lacquers the cars,
baleful reflections haunt the drunks
who stumble home from singles bars.

The singer's jeans are far too tight,
Cuban heels crucify his pigeon toes,
he's known as Billie in this town
where even weather is ambiguous.

The band gulp one tight-arsed beer,
slag-off his lipstick and sexual mime,
plot to sack him for strutting like a tart,
drifting out of key and out of time.

They won't see him sashay from the Gents
in a sable coat and thigh-high dress,
won't see the glitter on his cheeks
or hear his high heels' SOS.

They hump the gear and load the van,
drive off to takeaways, fierce Vindaloos,
or to a fumbled fuck from girls
who saw a bar-room stardom in their looks.

The singer watches in the glass,
he blows a kiss towards his face
and all those nights that lie ahead,
their unknown planes of time and space.

Their cigarette smoke is not yet burned
and mouths have not yet slurred out cheers
or tasted the lips of unkissed girls
or the virgin heads of unpulled beers.

Those hands he sees have not yet traced
the thickening waist of middle-age
or clapped him from his robes of silk
to preen onto the strobe-lit stage.

Dull days turn in half-forgotten towns
but each performance kills their death,
it's all to come – the glitz, the glam,
the shadow not yet pressing on his breath.

Bidean Nam Biam

Here the road shimmers into the day's
tide of heat, taking the tourists away
to pry at curios of tartan, brooch-pins,
the rusted blood of Highland feuds.

Pipers quarrel in the car park
at Glencoe, their Strathspeys
and reels strut out, clashing faintly
above birch leaves, the clucking
water in this gully;
its rocks are crampon-scarred
though most snow is gone –
just that pale cravat tucked
into the corrie's throat ahead.

The air is thick here,
trees exhale a chest-tight damp,
granite glimmers, choking the valley
with its unpronounceable history.

Above us, peaks vibrate to struck
notes of summer heat;
our tongues swell in mouths that
have nothing to say except curse
the angles of rock, this mad glare flinching
our eyes where the snow-slope begins.

We toil up it, touching its illusion
of cold, staring at the sun through the sting
of sweat and sun-cream, staggering its last
groove through an avalanche of light.

Five ravens circle the summit;
their cries fall from throats of bone,
their plumage shines then tilts
into blackness.

The loch's iris of white sand sifts
into its hourglass eye – a prophet's
burned out pupil, blinded to futures
that falter from our minds' certitudes.

A skylark sings briefly then falls;
the sky's blueness hums in electric
gatherings of light, in crackling gusts
of static, in a vacuuming momentousness
that the grass makes ordinary at our touch.

A breeze laps at us then gutters
into massed horizons where the mountains
stare us down, asking to be named;
the shock of the rock's stored heat
is a hand put suddenly in snow,
an insect zings by, gleaming
in its war-gear.

Thirst and silence have stilled
all thoughts but one:
to reach the ridge below, to fall
into the cool stare of the lochans,
into the corrie's shadow, hugged
close as unspent breath, covetous
as a dark conscience.

Descent is a treachery of skipping
stones and dust, it's a mirage
of cold beers lined at the bar,
buckets of ice, draught darkness,
bubbles rising into white necklets
of foam through which our mouths
would sink to drown this skidding
into unremitting waves of light.

We drink the rock's resolution
into rock and more rock and more
until we're plunging over bogland
to gulp our heads at the burn's jacuzzi,
swallowing its snow-melt cold,
its stinging effervescence,
scooping its joy of ice,
saying how we'd made it
and never thought we would,
how Christ's climb to Calvary
could not have been harder in such heat.

But the mountain isn't listening.

Our breath hollows out its silence,
our ears balance on their stirrups
of bone, predicting scree's slide
towards another winter.

I'm asking you what it means,
that name on the map, those words
clumsied as your mouth translates
a mountain to the English tongue –
Bidean Nam Biam –
meaning highest, meaning peak
of the mountains, meaning summit
which we've hardly begun
to understand we do not know.

Fox

The fox in the headlights
knows it shouldn't be here,
caught on the road through
the larch wood, just stepping
out to the chicken coop.

The fox is skittish;
it's made a *faux pas*,
executes a sorry jump
from pointed toes – a ginger
novice in the dancing class.

This is a thin fox caught
in sharp light, nervously
swishing the white tip
of its tail, painting itself
out into the dark.

A few strokes and it's gone
into a chiaroscuro dusk;
it shouldn't have been there
on the road, in this poem –
dancing, up to no good.

The Dream of the Circus Dwarf

I crouch in sawdust and lion shit,
watch the crotch of the new girl
glitter on the high wire
and chew my tongue like a dog;
the crowd fall silent, the apes
are lewd in their cage of laughter.

The lights are searching for her,
sweeping out that smoky canopy
where she has vanished and the wire
gleams, impossibly fine.

Now she shimmers from the ladder's
last rung, somersaults, takes her bow,
elusive as a trick with handkerchiefs
or a magic box or a smiling woman
sawn in half; she slaps her thigh,
passes me in this pit of shadow,
spits back their gaudy applause.

She sweats garlic, scowls often,
fucks hungrily behind the caravans,
taking a new man each night
and every one hare-lipped or limping –
even the Russian hunchback's had her.

This way, it makes her perfect.

One day she came as I threw fish
to the seals, dragged her hand
down my tattoos – the blue swan
on my wrist, the black snake
at my shoulder – put her mouth
to my back and breathed on me
as you'd breathe to polish silver
or a glass to peer through.

I dropped the bucket's dead shoal
into the pool and fled.

I am my own master:
there'll be no caressing me,
no petting of my body – she'll
tire of loose fucking first,
of losing herself in the dark gap
between guylines and brooms,
stuffing her shirt lap in her mouth
to come shuddering and gasping
like an expert, an artist.

She's watching me take water
to the elephants; her face
is young, her nipples hard
as buttons when she brushes
against me, imploring.

She sees me reading my almanac,
marking the map of Ursa Major
with purple ink, she follows
me outside to ask me what I see
beyond the awnings and the road,
beyond the stars' chart turning,
the hills' anvil beating
up dawn's smoke of cloud.

She asks me what I hear when
I put my head to the ground
and lie listening at the earth,
what I weep for when I weep
for the exile of this life –
what I might have been or am.

Tonight Mars enters Leo;
I'll sleep with that planet's
brand burning in my ribcage,

dream her high-stepping grace
through all its scarlet fogs.

I am the rod of correction
in her hands: pliant, slim
as a stoat's whisker, quivering
in the hushed trembling
of her steps upon the wire.

Their faces are upturned to
watch us, dim and rapturous;
her eyes level me at the horizon
where it spins below the night,
she flexes her thighs, squeezes
damp palms, pulls in her belly,
steps out where only I can
keep her from the space
hollowed by that fuming light.

A House of Glass

FEVER WARD

This house is so many windows tall.
I stare through its frosted panes
at an ice-dusted world, so sharp
so brittle I could snap it with one
finger's touch.

If I try to leave, their words
and hands will bring me back,
their kind words, their clean hands
smelling of soap and godliness.

Today a dead fox lies by the roadside,
its curled flame extinct in the gutter,
cobwebs trap the dawn in tattered lace,
the last flies are mummified.

Today these fossils of cold
are glazed upon the windows
for my breath to melt away.

The sun is low and white,
hallucinating at the horizon,
the whole world gone to mist
or to the bad for all I know.

At the zebra crossing that woman
takes the children across
to safety, her plastic coat
is white, her moon-eyed
spectacles are gleaming blanks;
she beckons but I will not go.

Last night I heard rain again,
each polished droplet breaking on
my throat, each cool tongue licking
at my breasts and neck.

I dream of aeroplanes falling
from the sky, planting bodies
in all the lawns, their flesh
a cold and bloody grimace
against those blades of green.

I awake to a house of glass,
to the hum of blood in my head,
the surgical smell of spirit
thinning the air.

I hear far-off rain, the high tide
in my head's shell, see new shores
pushing from your shoulders' pale
undulated curves of skin.

I am the hot tide tracing them,
trying to wear them away,
I want you to be white sand
in the furnace of my arms.
I'd fuse you to transparency
and lie inside your captured light.

I want to sleep away this heat,
this febrile sickness.
I want to be cold, insensible,
folded into sleep and dreamless
as a snowdrop is folded and dreamless
when it meets the night.

BLUEBELLS

It was after your call to come
and stay, the first time,
that amazing blue glimpsed
from the train, the miles drumming
past and dazing me with landscapes
too flat and sky-high for my head.

Those woods flashing wild volts
of bluebells, then swift clearings
then shadow, the glimmer of birch trees
pale as the legs of running girls.

The sun touched everything
with its styptic glare,
the horizon so low and hard
that just looking hurt.

At one station a thrush puffed
its breast from the signal
and the fuzzed hair of schoolgirls
filled with sun; they lifted their
bags and chattered into the carriage,
riding so bravely and blindly towards
the futures mapped for them.

Then a group of French teenagers
all around me, writing letters home,
their *sang froid*, their easy laughter
and affection and the woods still
going by in shocks of light.

Between my lips and the window glass
that song going round and round –
*just the thought of you
turns my whole world misty blue –*
turning and turning, easy and banal
but prefacing some great eventfulness.

Then stepping down, tight-chested
when you met me at the station,
your coat unbuttoned, your kiss
on my cheek quite neutral,
but under my hair your mouth
on my neck as we hugged,
your hands already searching
for me, right or wrong.

Then laughing a little meekly,
climbing into your car
which the sun had warmed
and your breath had scented
like yeast or new bread.

Then driving to your parents' house,
wanting to cry for the pleasure
of you and being together,
but looking straight ahead
at the traffic instead, hearing
you telling me what to do,
what to say.

FEVER

I am dry-lipped,
restless in the bed's
starched white acre.

A nurse brings a glass of water –
it is all tremors like ice melting
and cracking under gin's juniper sting.

There is sweat basting
my body. It makes this bed
smell of you, though
you are not here.

Your tread is gone
from the floor,
your bicycle we joked
was a man's
gone from the hallway.

Your tongue has sealed me
like an envelope written
with your address and only yours.

I remember that time you went
away, leaving me for days,
counting the minutes and hours,
undressing alone, the wardrobe
dark and shirtless where
I stood wondering
why I'd come
or what for,
reaching out to spook
the wire hangers, feeling
that draught of camphor
cool my thighs.

All night the lawns exhaled heat,
poppy heads were sticky
to split with seed, then
the moon was at the curtains,
tearing the edges of the clouds'
billet doux, plumping your empty
pillows with light.

REMISSION

Rain pries again at the window
furling the petals of lilac
and broom, chilling the vinegar-
scented glass where my breath lingers.

It clears and vanishes;
outside a blackbird chokes
on warbles of saturated air.

I touch this book, breathing
the print of your fingers from
the must of Faulkner's first novel,
seeing you scrawling your name
on the flyleaf in a tweed jacket
at some bookstall, the city's din
flowing around you and away
into the stillness of this moment
that is never really still.

I shrug off the memory I've
imagined, shudder
in my lambswool cardigan,
finger the pearl in my ear,
watch a droplet of rain sag
from the ruin of spiders' webs.

Everything is still so hard to grasp
or bear, so changed by heat,
my body's fury burning the days
to dross.

I sing five notes, placing them
precisely in the air;
they are footsteps climbing
the scale's even temperament,
ascending to an an overcast heaven.

Then sun is licking suddenly
at clear flames of rain,
stoking the bitter green furnace
of the hawthorn tree
where it signals at the window,
beaching the hours and wrecking them.

I put the book down, let
false memories lie their way
into my head, stare at the whorls
of my handprint where they circle
on the cold glass, taking me inward.

ALLOWED HOME

Today I am home, allowed
to be here where light is misting
the fields' green, twisting
like smoke in a crystal
and burning up the future.

Rivers conspire in the valley,
telegraph poles crucify the hills'
far off Calvary of grey;
beyond the iron railings
traffic labours in low gear,
a horse clops into the afternoon,
its whinny shivering the still air.

This morning I found a thumbprint
on the toothpaste; it could have
been yours. Could have been.
The taste of it was the taste
of you leaving – that day when
the car spun on a slick
of blackened ice and your head
starred the windscreen to enter
what lies beyond each and every
fragile house of glass.

We suspected nothing.
The night before I'd turned
you over like a new leaf
and couldn't get enough.

I wanted to flute your body's
fine reed, make each cry splutter
and rise into your throat
until they came clear as octaves
or perfect fifths.

I wanted us to mint our mouths
with cool lies for the world,
to fall into the space between your
voice and mine and never stop.

Never stop: half my head
is gone, I'm half blinded by days
that never seem to stop falling
into failed parabolas of light;
it's a fever, this life of waiting
for nothing, its minutes and hours,
its migraine close by and stunningly white.

Listen:
a pheasant is chinking two stones
in the copse below the house,
its brazen throat calling to make love,
to make it hot and quick with no regrets.
Its steady eye will seize the chance –
right or wrong –
and not reproach itself with tears.

But the sky is empty of birds.
They're too afraid to fly – fearful
of the hawk, or that tangle of wires.

I would not be.

The waterfall is hushed, yet still
it carries something forward, some
unseen sorrow that will arrive
in the present moment, never expected,
never, but here all the same.

I have the shape of your thumb,
its hollow to warm with mine
as rain spots the window quite
unhurriedly.

It will drench everything –
those faintly yellow leaves,
that dead ash tree, even the night
where it falls across my face,
careless, absent-minded as a kiss
half-tasted or not meant.

Moonwalking

Tonight I'm walking darkside,
tightroping this abyss of weightlessness
like a womb-walking child wanting

to somersault on its umbilical
and not quite daring; never nearer
yourself than here, nor further away.

You step into this tranquillity of dust –
silence of the thud of a choked tongue
booting your footsoles –

and the moon is all stillness,
has forgotten the catechism of life
which these steps are declaiming,

going nowhere. This lunar night
will not let words about their purpose –
they float free and airless

describing only godlessness.
Stars chime like ice in a tumbler,
yet there is no water here; the speech

of my heart runs backwards to a green day
when I followed a blackbird into woods
and a girl lay naked for me, touching

her eyelashes to my hot skin.
That slow rasp of breath is mine,
its silver chain of bubbles

entering the vacuum of each moment
which it cannot hold.
I scuff my feet in moon-dust,

the tongue's thirst for nameable
things: the earth, its blue
face of continents and seas, its white

axles of ice, and somewhere a house
in a town in crop-quilted fields
where I belong, or did, and once

gathered acorns in an autumn wood
where the same girl was walking,
though a woman now with children

at her hands, and tired, wilting
like something I'd picked and wasted
as a fool does, not meaning to.

Here the echo of starlight arrives
just as helplessly, travelling
from the beginning of light and time

because it has to, everything out there
already gone or changed, everything
mutable in brilliances that each probe

brings nearer by stepping further away.
I can't imagine infinity –
that mass of stars above my head

sings into the vaulting of space
and panics me like the screams
of swallows trapped and gone blind

in the mind's cathedral.
What calms and stills them in their
proper place – like bird-song in a wood –

is blindness itself, the love
we can't prevent ourselves from feeling,
our eyelids closing as we kiss,

our fingers reading in skin's sudden
blush of sweat everything that has
or can or will ever happen.

Machair

Sky is widest here, the sea
coldest against that dream of sand,
its white cuticle curving away.

A sycamore turns pale,
it sways like a tall woman
helplessly dancing.

A buoy rots in the marram,
luring that wrecked hull,
that tractor buried in pebbles

to its surf of rust.
Meadows of clover and buttercup
crumble at the beach where dunlin

feed, frenetic as roaches.
The tide hauls ropes of weed,
plovers call out with larks

and meadow pipits –
a multitude that could be heavenly
but the looted crofts, the undug

lazybeds say otherwise.
Uist men drive cattle in Paraguay,
steer cargoes out from Cape Breton,

the Gaelic snagging their tongues
with names and custom, tattered
as feedbags on barbed wire.

The waves drag at beer-cans,
sea-boots, a torn fishing net,
boiler-plates tumble in the backwash

and a Bedford van slips on the cliff.
Last night a seal came like a lost
dog to watch the land for humans

and found us, trudging at the machair,
trying to match oyster catchers' cries
with wrong words, the wrong language.

Remembering Dunblane's Children Derwentwater, March 1996

A still day with sun still buffing
each metal chuckle of the lake,
a day with doves clucking, waves
tonguing shoreline stones under
the delicately hymning wind.

A day where a stake is hammered
onto its own echo like something
vital being said about the day,
about sawn beech boles that still
glimmer through the standing trees.

Here the rock's leaves are pressed
close as pages in a book, heated
then twisted, then blackened
like pages in a burning book.

A goose trails its broken wing,
drinks the lake's long memory of cold,
snow still melting on the hills –
Skiddaw and Bleaberry Fell –
still melting our uplifted eyes.

Daffodils usher past the winter leaves
and though song is falling everywhere
we cannot count the birds or songs of birds,
their names or places where they fall.

Keswick town is quiet in the sun, intent
on busyness that keeps its resolutions
ticking on and something else at bay –
the thought that what is moving might be
still and letting life slip by instead.

A moorhen dips for weed, a line
of kayaks lifts the water's hem
where children have laid out jetties
of the smoothest stones, then stepped
off into a faint blue mist of permanence.

Valentine

Today I burn a mouse for you,
burn it because you rose early
and found it already dead
on the bathroom floor –
unexpected and frightening you said –
dozing again, that way you have of
talking in your sleep and waking me.

A small task; I give this mouse
to the shrivel of flame and smoke,
no stigmata on its hands, no sweat
of forgiveness or ironic vines across
its holy brow, but this mouth-shaped
wound in its side cannot be ignored
and bleeds like hidden kingliness.

Today I burn a mouse for you, burn it
like a late-fallen leaf, wondering
at the moment of its death, tripping
over spring's doorstep into sudden winter;
let our hearth mourn this the only way
it can – with heat, purifying fire,
with sulphur in its saffron temple.

A mouse dies unexpectedly, frightening
all the clocks in the house, which mutter
like footsteps over pontoon bridges,
out of step in case the whole thing fails;
take it, you said, *take it*,
these words somehow more distinct
than anything, so much clearer
than prayers I can't remember or recite.

Today I burn a mouse for you, burn
it in the stillness of this house
where the pipes murmur and light rises
at the windows, where you still dream
its sly scamper and rodent mirth,
its paws in the butter dish or
scooping up a manna of spilled oats
or weaving a nest in the sofa-back.

Today I burn a mouse for you
and only smoke slips between us
like the vaguest word for love.

Wardlock

The priest slides iron in my brass
mouth; he slips the bolt, tucks
the key into his soutane sleeve
then leaves to give the Sunday mass.

I am a hard heart – steel tumbler, pin –
I guard the letters she wrote
to his English address, their scent
sweating on his hands like sin.

I clamp the lid of oak veneer
this box his Irish father gave to him,
never imagining unpriestly things
concealed beyond confession's fear.

Her letters sigh in polished wood,
remembering the harvest dance:
his mouth so soft against her breasts
and moistness that she hardly understood.

I am neat and clever as a closing rhyme,
the perfect foil for unrequitedness,
the eunuch mechanic who cannot feel
or even cynicise this locking up of harm.

Every finger leaves its oxidising print,
his housekeeper polishes their tarnish off,
he lifts the host and sips the wine,
obedient tongues line up, as pink as lint.

He's laid these letters down too many years,
their bouquet's fading into dust,
their sweetness has acidified, souring
sentiments she wrote when pricked by tears.

I am the lock on all he never said,
the yielding replies he never sent,
rehearsed each night he spent alone
pinned tight by sheets on his seminary bed.

I am the guardian of his penitential cell,
I am its heavy slab of lead,
I am the moral and the prayer,
the brassy warning of its bell.

I am his knees' bone locked to floors,
his heart's late knocking at unopened doors.

Mannequins

Too late when ice has zinged
and parted with a splitting creak,
your face clutched blubbering under its
blurred cinemascope of sky, its green
trees bending over green water.

Too late when news has curled
and blown away from the table with
other trash and bad breath to the street,
the important things you meant to read
unread and unimportant yesterdays.

Too late that feather in your throat, that hand
on its way to her shoulder like a letter
lost in a mail-train some thugs derailed
or shunted into unlit sidings
where the signal weeps shattered glass.

Too late when her shoe cracks the window
and she's fighting free, scratching your face –
you bastard, bastard – when she's pulled
the car door shut, gunned the engine,
left tail-lights smouldering bad blood.

Too late the rope, gun, paracetamol
or fist, too late your lips frozen
at the bottleneck, the taste of whiskey-sick,
the headache pulsing at your hacked-off scalp,
the shivers at what you've done or not.

Too late now to put down old habits
of hopelessness, dress for the day,
open a window, let the cold creep
in like poisoned gas, too late to shun
postmen's messages or knuckle-dusting repo men.

Things get faster, go for broke, things spin –
the fuckers – spin and bite, their gear teeth meshing,
pulling you by the skin of yours into the days,
too dizzy, too late to smooth lapels
and nonchalantly grin and make an entrance,

too late to vote other futures home –
their winning smiles pipping good-natured
losers at the post – losers are bastards
anyhow and stink the way you do of something
closer than body odour or unclean sex.

These are your faces in the windows walking
towards you, a walk you know and recognise
like the faces of tomorrow, the slow tread
of bad luck or giros dropping in the hall,
these mannequins screaming in the shopping mall.

Hysterectomy

These streets when mist comes down
flurrying late snow out of hills where light
is ambushed, disappearing the parish church's
black anachronistic hull; these streets
and me, home again because my mother's
breath is fluttering under theatre lights,
the surgeon's mask, my father's anxiety
to brew incessant tea which he lays out
beforehand like a battle-plan – spoon, teapot
and kettle primed for every contingency but one.

I was here in '68 in spring, this market
hall before it burnt down and got rebuilt,
a teenager dreaming sex with girls in hot
rooms, these streets running downhill
from the mill's wall of glass; right here
at the ironmonger's stall sipping Vimto
as Russia invaded Czechoslovakia, shots
cracking over the tannoy and me walking
on into the next day and the next.

These streets, Jan Palach burning for freedom,
those Buddhist monks dying in Vietnam
newsreels; no girls, no sex in overheated rooms,
but napalm and prayer wheels and Mylai
and now my mother's breath straying out
from her body and back like a child that won't be told.

Today I'm drinking cappuccino in Burger King,
sipping this moment I'll never taste again,
watching a man spit at the new plaza, that
old woman drinking carton milk and stinking
of neglect, those two mothers prising kids
from Postman Pat's red van.

I don't yet know that later I'll pass
my old Latin teacher in the shopping mall,
unshaven, trembling with senile joy,
dragging his shopping bag behind him
like all the Latin I never learned –
except one passage that stuck, about
a woman and a girl in a wood, using
some vocabulary and grammar, its verbs
never quite managing to say what happened
to them back there in another century.

My mother's breath hovers like maidenflies
over the surface of her years, these streets
changed and sobered now, even the names
of pubs changed as if I should be shamed
by memories of drunkenness, of blurred
lights on the road below that took me home
to a terraced street, the morning cup of tea
putting down its question for discussion
of where I'd been and when, with whom.

Her breath hovers over and under everything:
these streets where all's for sale
and cheaper than it should be – like life,
itself, whatever that is – the young beautiful
in their ignorance, the old faltering past
wisdom to plots in the sea-grassed field
below the church that planners will build on
one day when back-handers are hinted
at drinks parties in the new town hall.

These streets, my sons, you'll read about
one day and maybe visit in their changes
when I'm not here – all changed except
for smells of grilled bacon and stale beer –
these streets where you'll know I loved
that moment when a man gobbed scorn
and mist took away the bus-station

then brought it back quite calmly,
dropping snow on my shoulders, the
sleight of its white hand onto a new coat
of cloth my father fingered and approved.

Too bad it doesn't really matter where I was
in '68 or where those girls were or what they
dreamed as that boy doused himself with petrol
for something always out of reach; these streets,
my mother's breath alighting daintily under
the surgeon's sterilising eye, his blade taking
away her womb like Dubcek to the Kremlin.

At home one day, you'll idly lift a book
you know I wrote, or having heard of Prague
in '68 read how I took her tulips and laid
them on the bed, then how she gave away
their pleasure like a bitter smile, still
wrapped and smouldering in their flames,
to an insincerely grateful duty nurse.

They were only flowers, you'll say
finding their crimson easy to picture,
but harder to see your grandfather scanning
the newspaper with thick glasses, or how
when I came home from town where no one
knew me anymore, snow melting on my coat,
the teapot stood ready and two cups, and
one white tea-bag smoothed out like a pillow.

The Hurts

TO LETHE ON THE 8-10

A weak dawn drowns all England under mist,
this train rocks us in its glass cradle
against the track where steel wheels hiss,
a slick of water glimmers on the pylons' cable.

Trees stand out as skeins of blackened wire,
the windows show us staring at our faces,
mist spreads, choking out the sun's ash-fire,
the stations' names christen nameless places.

That young couple are joined hand in hand,
he sleeps against her and she strokes his head,
he wakes to see pale fogs inhale the land,
white grasses that the winter leaves for dead.

The girder bridge flits by like a lantern show,
the river drinks our lights in darkness far below.

OCTOBERSCAPE

Last night was breathless here, trees
dropped their leaves in dusky stillness
sheer as the underslip silking your knees
or the inheld gasp of my caress.

Today the path is a dross of sycamore's
yellow stars, the woodland burns
with beeches, a soot of crows floats
above their flames and slowly turns.

The air is indrawn, so still a film of dust
scums the lake where coot and mallard dive,
trees rustle naked, their sound so soft
it intimates our whispered cries of love.

Last night you wept and threw your shoe against my face,
today I search for where we lay but cannot find the place.

RED SHIN COVE

Holy Island glimmers faintly to the south,
its silver mirage trembles under wind
that raises sand to sting our mouths
and bury footprints that we leave behind.

Two girls play, half-naked in the sea,
cormorants fly low, terns dive then
wavecrests fling them to my searching eye,
this beach is ground from creatures once alive.

A tanker passes slowly, heading east to
where the sky has dunked itself in blues,
the waves ferment against our feet, their yeast
of salt will dry and whiten on our shoes.

At dusk I'll light a fire of driftwood in the sand,
pour broken shells and promises into your hand.

AXE

The axe speaks clearly to the wood,
its steel tongue thuds along the grain,
the halves drop cleanly if the line is good
and if the head is truly aimed.

This log has knots where offshoots grew,
the axe falls, stammers, then sticks.
My wrist is numbed through – blood to bone –
though it should be wise to timber's tricks.

You're watching from the window with our child,
your lips leafing a brief, subtle smile,
each dumb blow entangles me, until I've used
up every angle, all my guile.

The verbs and nouns of steel will never part
a wood so knotted, inarticulate.

BURN MOOR

Night has scorched the heather roots ash white
and every rock is pale with crystal dust,
cold has hulled the tarns, all night
fixing plates of ice, rivets of frost.

The purple hills are vague, seem to burn
beyond this mist that we are stumbling in,
adders are asleep beneath these stones,
veiled in the venom-diamonds of their skin.

The quaking bog's a frozen crust of grass
where grouse's wings explode their panic-blur,
wind goads us speechless with its lash,
sky sloughs the sun – a moon's faint replica.

Frost crystals blow and hiss upon the stones,
we turn for home and find our footprints gone.

ALONE

You're three days gone away – at first the space
you left was small and I was free inside it,
now that you're coming back, your hands, your face,
your eyes invade my sleep and wake me

to this absence. Cold has whitened all the roofs,
which the sun licks damp and black, a fire-cat
lapping up the sleeping town where proof that we
exist at all is scarce as letters on the mat.

No letters come, no sad voice shimmers
down a cackling line – too far away, too lost
for that. I dust your shoes, polish off last glimmers
of the window's funeral-parlour leaves of frost.

The hours between us are dull sleepers, they let pass
steel lines, your train, you dozing in its chrysalis.

WORDS

Words wait, just as minerals sleep in stone
to be washed out slowly by the rain,
their crystals interlock and they alone
can articulate the facets of our pain.

They glint in sun's temporary light,
the brief visitation that lets bloom
Earth's breathing green, our own delight
in words that even humanise a sterile moon.

Each brilliant syllable in space
will turn and fall dumb to the light,
every kiss I'll ever burn into your face
will cool and fade. You'll forget tonight

but it doesn't matter, we'll die anyhow,
it matters that we feel the hurt of loving now.